99.2
MEA

DATE DUE

THE DOMINIE WORLD OF ANIMALS

KOALAS

Graham Meadows & Claire Vial

Contents

Dominie Press, Inc.

About Koalas

Koalas belong to a group of mammals called marsupials. The difference between marsupials and other mammals is that female marsupials, such as koalas and kangaroos, carry their young in a pouch.

Koalas in the **wild** are found only in the forests of eastern Australia. The largest koalas are found in the south, where it is cooler. They have dark, thick fur and shaggy ears. Koalas that are found further north, where it is warmer, are smaller, and their fur isn't as shaggy.

Where They Live

Koalas are excellent climbers. They live, eat, and sleep high up in eucalyptus trees, where there are plenty of leaves for them to eat. The leaves help to protect them from the hot sun and the rain. They also hide the koalas from **predators** such as owls and eagles.

Koalas are **nocturnal**. That means they are active at night. They spend up to nineteen hours a day sleeping, usually lying or sitting in the branches of trees. While they sleep, they stop themselves from falling by holding on with their legs.

Where They Live

Except for mothers with their babies, koalas like to live alone.

Most koalas live in a certain area of trees. This area, called their home range, is usually smaller than eight acres. Females and males can share the same home range. If two or more koalas share the same tree, they live in different branches of that tree.

Koalas mark the trees and leaves in their home range with their scent, or special smell. This lets other koalas know that they live there.

Koalas **communicate** by making noises such as **bellows**, screams, grunts, and growls.

Their Shape and Size

Adult koalas weigh between nine and thirty pounds and are two to three feet long. Their weight and size depend on where they live. Males are larger, heavier, and more muscular than females.

Koalas have short, thick tails. Their noses and ears are large. Their thick fur is waterproof and warm.

Male koalas live for about ten years in the wild. Females live up to fifteen years in the wild.

Their Feet and Claws

Koalas have sharp, curved claws to help them hold on to tree trunks and branches. They have thick pads on all four feet. A koala's feet are specially designed for climbing. The first toe on their back feet is shaped like a thumb. The second and third toes are joined together.

Koalas can jump short distances from one branch to another, or from one tree to another.

Their Diet

Koalas are **herbivores**, which means they eat only plants. Eucalyptus leaves are the main part of a koala's **diet**. There are more than 600 types of eucalyptus trees. Koalas eat the leaves of about fifty of these different types.

There is poison in the new leaves of some eucalyptus trees. Koalas have an excellent sense of smell. They can tell which leaves contain poison just by smelling them. Before they eat a leaf, they check it by smelling it.

An adult koala eats more than two pounds of leaves, buds, and stems every day.

Their Diet

Koalas like to eat fresh, green shoots, or new leaves, that grow on each type of eucalyptus tree for just a few months a year. This means they have to keep moving from one tree to another in order to feed on fresh leaves.

If the trees are close together, the koalas climb from tree to tree. But if the trees are far apart, they climb down to the ground and walk to the next tree. While they are on the ground, they are in danger of being attacked by predators.

Koalas will travel a mile or more in search of tasty food.

When They Mate

Koalas start to **mate** when they are about three years old. The mating season is during the Australian spring and summer.

Male koalas often gather a group of two or three females to form what is called a harem. Koalas are usually peaceful animals. But during the mating season, males sometimes fight to protect their harems. The males grunt to attract females. Male koalas growl at each other when they are fighting.

Koalas mate at night, high up in the trees.

Their Young

Most female koalas give birth once every two years. Usually only one baby is born at a time, about five weeks after the female has mated. Baby koalas are blind and hairless when they are born. They are less than one inch long!

After it is born, the baby koala crawls through its mother's fur and finds its way into her pouch. Once it is inside the pouch, the baby holds on to its mother with its mouth. It breathes through its nose while it **suckles**, or drinks its mother's milk.

When it is about seven months old, the baby koala pokes its head out of its mother's pouch for the first time.

Their Young

About a week after the baby koala first pokes its head outside, it climbs out of its mother's pouch. Once it comes out of the pouch, it holds on to the fur on its mother's stomach. At this stage, the baby is about eight inches long.

For the next four or five weeks, the baby koala climbs in and out of its mother's pouch. The pouch is safe and warm. Inside it, the baby can suckle and sleep.

Their Young

Soon the baby koala grows too big to get back into its mother's pouch. But it still puts its head inside the pouch to drink her milk. By this time, the baby is learning how to ride on its mother's back by holding on with its strong claws.

The baby koala is **weaned** when it is about eleven months old.

Young koalas leave their mothers when they are about two years old. When they are three, they begin to mate, and the koala **life cycle** begins again.

A koala reaches full size when it is about four years old.

Glossary

bellows:	Loud, deep noises
communicate:	To share information; to send a signal
diet:	The food that an animal or person usually eats
herbivores:	Animals that eat plants
life cycle:	The stages, or phases, of an animal's life
mate:	To join with another animal in order to produce offspring
nocturnal:	Active at night
predators:	Animals that hunt and kill other animals
suckle:	To drink a mother's milk
weaned:	No longer drinking a mother's milk; able to find and eat other food
wild:	Natural surroundings; not a zoo

Index

Publisher: Raymond Yuen
Editor: Bob Rowland
Designer: Carol Anne Craft

Photo credits copyright © 2000: Graham Meadows (cover and pages 2, 4, 6, 8, 10, 12, 14, 18, and 20). Photobank Image Library, New Zealand (pages 16 and 22).

Published by:

꒒ **Dominie Press, Inc.**

1949 Kellogg Avenue
Carlsbad, California 92008 USA

ISBN 0-7685-0966-1

Printed in Singapore by PH Productions Pte Ltd
1 2 3 4 5 6 PH 02 01 00

www.dominie.com